GUIDE TO WOMEN ORAL SEX

How to perform any type of oral as a lady and wow your male partner.

Dr. Jovany Steuber

Table of contents

Introduction

Going down, 'rimming' and 'blow jobs' are some of the various methods of describing oral sex. Oral sex involves using your mouth or tongue to lick, suck or stimulate your partner's genitals or anus.

Many people love oral sex, but it is a personal issue and not everyone enjoys it or chooses to perform it. There are many methods to offer or receive oral sex. You may opt not to have oral sex at all, or you may like trying it out with your spouse to find out what brings you both pleasure.

It is crucial to chat with your spouse about oral sex so you can understand what they enjoy and don't like. Every individual is different, so it might take a time to discover what makes someone feel good. The greatest thing to do is to maintain chatting with your spouse. Ask them to tell you what feels wonderful and let them know when you are enjoying something.

If you're happy and comfortable with someone, oral sex may be a terrific way to become physically closer and understand what turns each other on. If you realize you aren't enjoying anything, it's your right to quit at any moment you choose, and the same is true for your partner.

Chapter 1:

Why he loves oral sex

Most males enjoy blowjobs. And some females DON'T adore giving oral. But let's look into WHY males like oral sex so much and how it may lead to:

- A happy partnership
- A good relationship
- Less stress and fewer fights
- Better allocation of energy duties in the partnership
- Greater trust between you and your spouse

Men and women don't always understand one other. Because guess what? We are different!!
Men don't grasp these delicate creatures that they also love so passionately.

And women, well, let's be honest. Men aren't that hard to figure out. But you have to make the effort to understand what makes individuals tick. And then put those ideas into practice!

Ladies, read on and learn why giving your partner a BJ is one of the Best things you can do for your relationship.

If you want a man to utterly and completely commit to you, then this sort of sexual connection is going to improve the possibility of that happening to you. (In a relationship and wish to increase the connection between you and your partner?

Sign up for the Relationship Reconnection! Yes, it's free!)

Sound good?

And as a side note, I don't think most males would be able to tell you just WHY they like oral sex. They'd probably just say 'because it feels good.' Um, absolutely. We know that.

But let's go a little farther into the subconscious and energetic reasons why BJs encourage a man to commit to you honestly and totally.

7-reasons-why-men-love-bjs

Submissive Woman

The basic act of dropping down on your knees is one of submission. It's one of service. You are providing for your guy. You have to be vulnerable to him. You have to surrender to him. And for a strong macho guy, it communicates that you trust him. It helps him feel more like a macho person.

If you're actually down on your knees, you are effectively making yourself submissive to him. You're giving him the potential to dominate.

Vulnerability and Trust

Let's be truthful here. I wouldn't give a blow job to anyone other than my significant other.

Back in the day when I was dating... I remember having talks with females about proximity and sex. And one woman, in particular, stated that she wouldn't go 'with a guy but that they'd screw around and have oral. I remember being startled! There is NO WAY IN HELL I would put just ANY random-ass penis in my mouth. Sorry to be nasty but oral sex is all about vulnerability and trust.

You have to be open to your boyfriend. You have to trust him. You have to feel comfortable enough to speak and ask specific things like 'Does this feel good?' or 'like this?' or 'Faster or slower?'

The masculine energy wants to be trusted by his girlfriend. That is HUGE for the manly energy guy. When you go down on your partner, you are signaling that you trust him because you feel comfortable being fully vulnerable with him.

Admiration

Most males adore their penises. I haven't yet seen one who doesn't!

When you take in your mouth what most guys are 'in love with, the base of their manhood, you are telling your spouse that you adore him.

You appreciate the quality of him that finally makes him a man.

And on the other side, if you're rejecting your man's penis via oral sex, you are saying that you 'reject him' or that you don't love him.

Amazing how much connection arises from just one little action.

Love

There are lots of ways we provide and receive love: hugging, kissing, buying presents, going out to dinner at a nice restaurant, stroking, saying "I love you" and more.

And while there are different means to convey love, guys have a specific connotation with sex and love that is separate from women.

Have you ever questioned yourself: "Why is it all always about sex?"

Or at least heard a girlfriend ask it?

NEWSFLASH: Men LOVE sex.

Did you hear that?

They LOVE it. It's part of how they perceive love.

You've got to simply grab the sentence above and trust that it's real.

To a guy, if a woman wants to have sex with him regularly, it indicates she loves him and is attracted to him. The male energy feels substantial in a woman being sexually attracted to him. So when this magnificent creature to who he's very sexually attracted is likewise super sexually attracted to him.... he gets it. It's his language.

Oh and get this, ladies. When you have sex with your boyfriend, oxytocin is released. It's the feel-good hormone that bonds you to a man and makes you think you're in love. So this happens to us, too. This is also why you should be incredibly attentive about who you sleep with as you physiologically attach to them for up to 8 weeks!

Connection

Most guys don't open up and communicate their views and feelings as frequently as women.
Sex is one sort of connection for them because they don't generally go out and converse with their male buddies the way we women communicate with our companions.

Think about sex and orgasm for a second. Men experience orgasm and 'let go.' Usually, it suggests they fall asleep. They are letting go of all the stress and anxiety of the day. They have accomplished their mission and their objective.

For women, we experience climax and we want to 'hold on.' We want to snuggle. We want to debate this. We desire to deepen the connection. The holding on indicates how much more emotional we are than guys. We are very emotional creatures and don't NEED sex to have a connection to our partner.

Whereas, guys do NEED sex to feel a connection to us.

It's Feminine, Baby!

I've talked a lot about masculine and feminine energy. And that's because it's vital to grasp regards to a joyful and healthy partnership.

Opposites attract. Compliments repel.

You need one Fred and one Ginger if you're dancing.

And you still need one Fred and one Ginger if you're dancing between the covers.

Once the feminine energy starts to understand the male energy and his yearning for connection through sex, many impediments slip away.

The feminine energy is gratifying her desire to connect emotionally with her man.

The male energy feels respected and trusted.

And when the feminine energy has her feelings valued (which she wants at her core above all else) and the masculine energy has his thoughts acknowledged (which he wants at his core above all else) the connection evolves into something you've never experienced before!

It's just plain sexy

Men want to feast with their eyes. And it looks great when you have his manhood in your mouth. Men love to watch when you're going down on them (have you noticed?). So make a show out of it. Wear seductive undergarments. Position yourself in front of a mirror. Look up at him occasionally. He'll eat that garbage up! I promise.

Are blow jobs even more intimate than sex?

1. It feels quite wonderful.

There's something about being engulfed by the warm wetness of demanding lips that genuinely sets our pulse beating. "But don't you get the same sensation being cuddled into a moist vagina?" Yes... if your vagina has a tongue.

You see, oral sex is more of an ensemble piece than vaginal intercourse. A good blow job involves the coordinated participation of lips, tongue, saliva, hand, and — on very rare occasions — a responsive gullet. Tough for your nether regions to compete with such a well-oiled oral team.

2. It's practically stress-free for men
Unlike normal sex where the have to be concerned about being hard enough, massive enough, and long-lasting enough, "linguistic love" carries with it no such angst-inducing demands. The are free to relax and enjoy themselves knowing that their orgasm will arrive at the appropriate time - no matter how soon that is.

3. The voyeur in us has an opportunity to come into action.

Unless we have mirrors or video recording equipment in our bedroom, we rarely truly get to witness or feel sex when we are actively indulging in it. But with oral sex, we have the opportunity to witness you work your magic on our intimate parts.

We get to witness you delight us, which only further amplifies our enjoyment. It's like we're starring in our tiny pornographic film (and you know how much we love our nasty movies) (and you know how much we appreciate our filthy movies) (and you know how much we enjoy our dirty movies).

4. It's all about leisure - not procreation.
The objective is pleasure, not offspring. In other words, it's a chance to have a good time without the risk of 18 years of financial

commitment. It's orgasm without a price tag, and we appreciate that.

5. Your resolve to selflessly support us makes us feel confident.

You're catering to our needs without demanding anything in return. Thus oral sex is a present, of sorts — a tiny extra delivered lovingly to us by someone who wants nothing more than to make us feel good. And what's not to appreciate about that?

I am not, however, advocating that you must indulge in this sexual behavior to gratify your boyfriend. If the prospect of partaking in such an act repulses you — and your vagina has been sexually doing all the heavy lifting for years without complaints from your lover — then why alter what's not broken?

On the other hand, if you're seeking to spice up your sexual repertoire with a performance piece that's certain to win you a standing ovation from your man's sexual apparatus, then blow jobs are the ticket.

It's a great present for all occasions, and there's very little chance he'll want to switch it, re-gift it, or return it for store credit. There's no question about it, males adore blow jobs.

So am I advocating that you have to give your lover a blow-job every single day to attain long-lasting happiness in your relationship?

Well, maybe I am saying precisely that.

But if not, at least once a week!

I hope by now you have realized that it's more than only oral sex: it's respecting your partner, it's being vulnerable, it's developing your connection, it's trusting him, it's opening up to your pure feminine nature.

Chapter 2:

Importance of oral sex

Sexuality is a vital aspect of every good, well-balanced relationship. Sex serves to bring you closer in a manner that only romantic connections can encourage.

The value of sex is tailor-made in the individual relationship. Where, how, and how frequently you have it is absolutely up to the two (or more) persons in an intimate and loving relationship.

That being said, oral sex also plays a crucial part in good relationships.

Sexuality is not simply restricted to penetration. All types of sex are significant.

It might be tempting to slip into a pattern if you're established into a long-term relationship — skipping oral sex, exploration, and sex toys in favor of planned coitus — but you should attempt to prevent this.

Keeping things enjoyable and personal is crucial to creating a solid relationship between you and your spouse. Sex shouldn't be something you have to do, it should be something you want to do.

Oral sex shouldn't go by the wayside simply because you've found your rhythm with someone you truly love.

Oral sex is an excellent strategy to induce sexual compatibility.

Sperms may help you keep your skin young. Women who engage in oral sex more regularly are protected against breast cancer Oral sex...say what?

Using your lips, tongue, and fingers to stimulate your partner's genitals is defined as oral sex. This style of sex, which is typically done as part of foreplay, is an excellent method to activate sexual compatibility and find new sensations with your partner. Women may not like it, and men might constantly want to hasten it. But having oral sex is proven to offer various health advantages.

For instance, did you know that semen might aid women to overcome sadness, and even help in having bright skin? Lowering blood pressure, alleviating tension, and even lowering the chances of prostate cancer...all these are just a few of the examples which illustrate that engaging in oral sex works as a win-win scenario for both men and women.

Oral sex is incredibly excellent for healthy relationships and shouldn't be placed on the back burner and here's why

1. Helps in getting a better sleep

Semen includes melatonin, a hormone that stimulates sleep and calm. Even without having intercourse, it will enter your bloodstream and assist you to doze asleep better than normal.

2. Anti-aging

Sperm contains a molecule called spermidine, which assists in aging at a slower pace. Do not apply it on your face but simply swallow it. Research shows that it will benefit you in a much better manner than any other anti-aging lotion.

3. Lower risk of breast cancer

Post the age of 40, most women are prone to the hazards of breast cancer. Confirmed research suggests that women who engage in oral sex at least twice a week have reduced odds of breast cancer than others. Semen includes substances that hinder the development of this form of cancer.

4. Improves memory

For individuals who struggle with chronic memory loss and are overly reliant on their phone reminders...guess what! Oral sex has come to your rescue. Semen includes nutrients that help you perform more efficiently.

5. Pain alleviation

Semen includes oxytocin and endorphins that serve as pain relievers. So, the next time you have back pain, headache, or any form of physical ailment, go to your spouse and delight him/her with some foreplay and oral fun!

As it turns out, a man's sperm is nothing less than amazing. Oral sex doesn't seem so horrible anymore, right? After all, what's better than having delightful oral sex which promotes your health too?

6. There is no incorrect way to enjoy sexuality.
In a recent conversation with Emmalee Bierly, MFT, Jennifer Chaiken, MFT, and Caitlyn Caracciolo, MFT, the proprietors of The West Chester Therapy Group, they informed me there was no incorrect way to experience sexuality.

Meaning that a pair's comfort and sexuality are absolutely specific to that particular relationship. There will inevitably be one spouse who has a larger sex desire in a relationship. When this occurs, you have to establish a balance that will keep both individuals satisfied.

This is where oral sex can be such a beneficial technique. I've written about my massive sex drive throughout my literary career. My partner's sexual desire is not nearly as great as mine. If I need an orgasm and he isn't experiencing sex, he'll go down on me. It's a solution that works for us.

This won't be the situation for all couples. Some individuals could discover their sexual balance in various ways such as one partner using a sex toy on the more sexual partner or masturbating with the less sexual spouse behaving as an active participant. It's all about a personalized balance inside each relationship.

7. Oral sex might be more intimate than penetrative sex.
In my perspective, oral sex is so much more personal than penetrative sex. F*cking is a simpler act. You meet at a pub, go home, bang. Everyone experiences an orgasm (if you're doing it properly).

You can have casual sex and yet have an orgasm. In most circumstances, you can't offer a casual head and have an orgasm.

When you give someone a blow job or conduct cunnilingus, you're not gaining anything out of this encounter. To me, this demonstrates that you care about this individual. You give a sh*t about his or her satisfaction. Big f*cking deal, I'd think.

For some individuals, this is not the case, but for me, if I'm willing to go down on you, forgoing any opportunity of having an orgasm, it implies I care a f*ck about you. If this is a casual meeting, I'm simply seeking to f*ck and go home to eat snacks on my sofa alone.

8. Mutual sexual experiences assist to build connections.
When we have an orgasm, our bodies produce the "love hormone," oxytocin. It's a

feel-good neurochemical that helps you feel closer to your lover. Orgasms are required for mutual sexual enjoyment.

While orgasm is a reasonably normal side-effect of sexual activity for the cis-gendered male half of the population, for women it is a little more elusive. Seventy-five percent of women cannot attain orgasm by penetrative intercourse alone. Our clitoris wants stimulation. Oral sex entails a lot of clitoral activity and a lot of consequent orgasms. Orgasm on top of the "giving" component of oral sex will boost pair bonding with your spouse.

Sex of all forms is necessary for healthy partnerships. When you know your partner's body and take the time to get in touch with what makes them feel good, you'll boost your intimacy and your connection which will enrich your relationship as a whole.

I hope this gives everyone a reason to get some heads up tonight. God speed.

Chapter 3:

Positions to give the best oral sex

The finest sex positions for oral pleasure:

1.The 69

The 69 oral sex position demands you and your partner to arrange themselves on top of each other in opposing directions, allowing you each great access to each other's genitals. "Many find the dual pleasure tremendously sexy," adds Cline.

Usually, one partner sleeps on their back and the other lies atop them with their legs straddling the other person's head. No matter your gender or anatomy, the 69 is a superb oral sex position for women, including those who are interested in blowjobs positions.

However, this stance isn't without its (solvable) drawbacks. "The 69 position is rubbish for many individuals," Sweet explains. "It may be really difficult to retain the posture, and it can be highly distracting to both give and receive at the same time!"

Because of this, some couples explore this position by laying on their sides and facing their partner's genitals, which Cline says offers your neck a respite. Or they perform the 68, a version of the 69 where your spouse sleeps on their back while you lie on your back on top of them with your crotch in their face. From that perspective, you may tease your lover with controlled motions of your genitals via pressure, rhythm, and depth.

2.Sit & Kneel

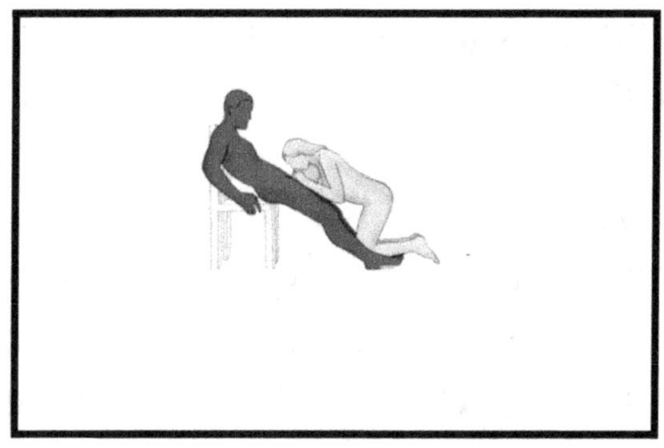

You sit; they kneel. Whether you attempt it to give a blowjob or stimulate a clitoris, the sitting oral sex position includes the receiver sitting with their pelvis at the edge of a chair, sofa, bed, kitchen counter, or other comfy surfaces while the provider kneels and pleases them orally.

To make this posture more pleasant, the provider might lay a cushion under their knees. And on the receiving end, persons with vulvas may lay their foot or leg on their partner's shoulder to create a deeper all-access pass to their genitals.

AASECT-certified and board-certified sexologist Jenni Skyler, Ph.D., LMFT, CST, says an upside of this position is "it also allows for a lot more mobility of both hands, so a spare hand can fondle the testicles or stimulate the vagina"—or partners can maximize each other's oral pleasure with internal or external sex toys for couples.

3.On Your Stomach

While you lay on your stomach, open your legs and arch your hips slightly so your lover may orally enjoy you from behind. (A cushion can help!) This oral sex position accommodates persons with vulvas, and you also have free range to enjoy yourself with toys or your hands at the same time. It's also wonderful for rim jobs. Because the donor isn't arching, lifting, or stretching their butt, this is a little more pleasant than doggie style, but they can still reach the same portions of the receiver's body.

4.The Classic

Just lay back and accept it. A wonderful and pleasant oral sex position for persons with penises or vulvas, this one is basic and straightforward: Lie back on a comfy surface (usually a bed or sofa) while your spouse lays on their stomach in between your legs and pleases you.

"The position is fantastic because it gives a lot of comfort for the provider and the recipient," Cline explains, adding that you may lay a cushion under your hips to enable better access to the places you want to be stimulated. Feel free to bend your legs, keep them flat on the bed, or wrap them over your partner's head.

5.Giraffe

There are numerous names for this oral sex position, but here's how you perform it: One partner sleeps on their back with their head going slightly over the edge of the bed. The second partner stands above them, bending forward so their crotch rests precisely on the bottom partner's lips.

You may try this facing your partner's body or face, but you might want to access the rest of their body for a sexy view and the potential to pleasure them.

This may not be the finest blowjob position for the providing partner since it's not particularly neck-friendly, but you can easily make it one of the top partners lowers the penis into their partner's mouth. Or if the bottom partner has a penis too, the top partner may suck them off at the same time, converting this upside-down position into 69.

6.Face-sitting

Sometimes termed queening, the face-sitting oral sex position is exactly as it sounds—one partner straddles the face of the other person, who may then lick, suck, or kiss their partner's genitals.

What's enjoyable and seductive about this posture is that it enables "the recipient to engage more interactively by grinding and rotating their hips," explains Cline. Plus, it "invites in a sense of control and surrender, which may be immensely sexy."

To make this a blowjob position, have the receiver sit at an angle and "feed" their penis into the giver's mouth to eliminate any neck stress or pain and the danger of asphyxia.

7.Doggy Style

Oral sex is excellent on all fours. Whether you lift your butt to attain doggy style or you balance yourself on your hands and knees, this is a worthy oral sex position that's feasible for penis-holders but likely more delightful for vulvas or ass-eating because of easier access.

As the recipient, you may open your legs to allow your partner's lips in deeper or keep them tight together to enjoy a real tease. When you've gotten into this position, the other person kneels behind you and stimulates your anus or genital region, either with their tongue or sex toys. (Or both!)

The cool feature of this position is you can both control the pace—they can decide the quantity of pressure they apply, and by sensually sliding your body forward and back, you can control how much of you they reach.

Pro-tip: While you or your lover receive, consider wearing a butt plug to heighten your enjoyment!

8. Standing Up

"Standing during oral sex may also be a terrific posture to establish a sense of authority," explains Cline.

In this posture, the receiver leans against a wall with their legs slightly apart and their pelvis stretched out, while the pleasurer kneels on the floor or sits. An oral sex position that works well for both vulva- and penis-havers, Cline claims couples can enjoy this one everywhere, from the bedroom to the kitchen to the shower to the pantry and beyond.

To protect your knees or theirs, don't forget the cushion. And to retain your balance (particularly when you come closer to having an orgasm), attempt to lean against a wall or door.

9.The Kivin technique

An oral sex position that works to deliver blowjobs and cunnilingus, the Kivin technique gives a sideways flare to the standard position. This one demands the receiving partner to lay on their back while the donor lies perpendicular to their partner's body. As the provider licks or sucks their partner's genitals, the receiver may drape a leg over their neck, which widens the legs further and promotes clitoral stimulation.

Tips & tricks

I.Protect your neck.
"First and foremost, be nice to your neck!" recalls Sweet.

In any oral sex position, she suggests making sure it doesn't create strain or discomfort in your body. If that occurs, shift positions. "The neck is quite vulnerable, and if the objective of the oral sex session is pleasure, be aware of discomfort in your performance."

You may always position a cushion beneath the pelvis, which she adds might be useful to raise your genitals, "providing better access and less neck strain."

II.Explore the rest of their body.

While you're pleasing your partner, don't hesitate to use your free hands to bring them added pleasure by softly tracing their breasts or nipples (nipple orgasms are a thing, and don't sleep on male nipple play!), grabbing or playing with their butt, gripping their waist, or anything you think your partner would enjoy. Because oral sex simply requires your mouth, you may be as flexible as you like to heighten your partner's enjoyment.

III.Use toys and props.

"Oral sex might be a terrific moment to bring in a toy—think of it as a collaborator for pleasure," says Cline. While your tongue can excite your partner tremendously, some numerous devices and toys make sex more delightful.

IV.Talk while doing it.

Communication is crucial for most things in life, including sex. "About all the roles, make sure you offer feedback with what you like and provide instruction about what you don't like," Cline adds.

V.Show your enthusiasm.
If you appreciate how your spouse tastes, let them know! Or if you like gratifying them, feel free to let a few groans out. Receiving pleasure appears thoughtless, but some individuals could overthink how they feel or taste or whether you genuinely appreciate giving them head. To both soothe their concerns and help them relax to better enjoy oral sex, show your partner how much their tastes and fragrances thrill you in ways that are authentic to you.

VI.Use your breath.
For some individuals, feeling their partner's warm breath on their skin during sex causes greater desire and may intensify the sensation. Whether you breathe forcefully and deeply while you delight their clitoris or you teasingly blow air on their skin, your

spouse is likely to be overcome with desire, particularly if you do this after a round of foreplay.

VI.Increase the closeness.
To strengthen your connection with your lover when you give them oral sex, heighten the closeness by holding their hands or locking eyes with them. Not only can witnessing your lover respond to your touch make sex sexier, but these intimate motions show them how much you want to feel them beyond just your lips. (Here are some additional methods to offer more intense oral sex.)

VII.Switch up your pace.
When you're licking, sucking, or caressing a vulva, bear in mind going straight into it might be overwhelming for a lot of folks. Starting softly with mild nibbles and licks is always encouraged, and then you may change to a speedier pace as your spouse reacts more and more to your stimulation.

Wrap your fingers around his shaft and stroke up and down as you kiss and suck his head or the top half of his shaft and head.

Use your hand to twirl his shaft so his head moves on the roof of your mouth and your tongue.

Squeeze and rub his head while tempting his shaft with your lips.

Your hands, particularly when well-lubed, may be an extension of your mouth and amplify the pleasure your mouth is bringing.

10.Comfy Blowjob

I have no issue with the "on your knees" blowjob position, but I know a lot of people who feel uncomfortable with the power dynamic inherent to that setup—so let's ditch that posture for now, and turn it into something more pleasant.

Have the partner having oral sex lie down on the bed or floor (preferably a carpet—nobody loves to give or receive head on frigid tiles) with their head put onto a pillow. The partner practicing oral sex may also lie down—but on their stomach—with their head between their partner's legs. (Face-to-balls or face-to-vulva, if you will.) The individual delivering oral sex may hold themself up as much or as little as they wish to employ their elbows and knees.

The Cozy Blowjob is exactly as pleasant as it sounds—and gives a beautiful view to everyone involved.

11. Sideways 69

69 is a classic for a reason, but it could be scary if you've never tried it before. By shifting the posture sideways, you experience the same reciprocal stimulation with none of the dangerous suffocation—plus, it's just easier for everyone concerned.

Start by resting on your side, facing your partner's genitals. Have them do the same. You may lift your leg and wrap it around your partner's neck or body to draw them closer in and intensify the pressure.

12.Sitting Down and Going Down

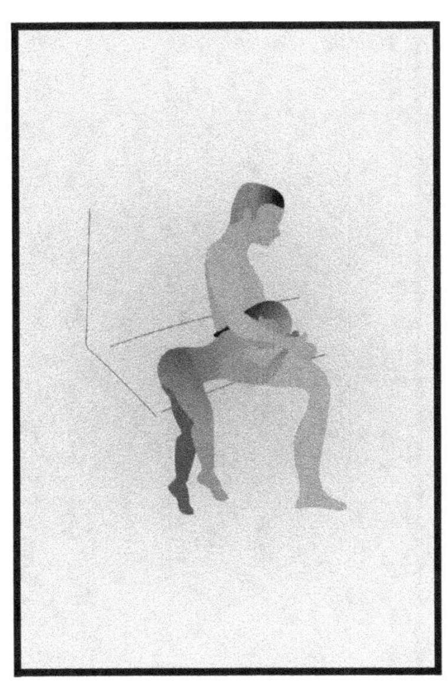

Blowjobs are hard work! Why not sit down while you're at it? Start by sitting side-by-side on the couch with your sweetheart, then take turns performing oral sex in a "road head" stance. (And please do this instead of ever executing true road head.) This can be a fantastic way to interrupt a calm day while watching TV and throw a little excitement into the mix.

13. The Side Sit

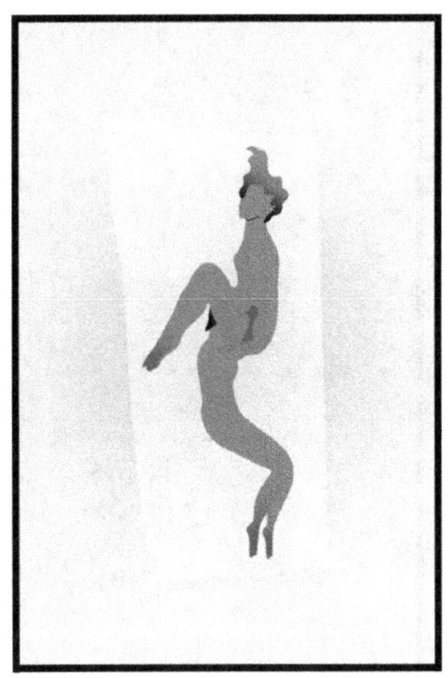

The usual cunnilingus position—where the receiving partner lies down on the bed, legs spread—can appear enormously scary, almost vulnerable. If you're not comfortable having a person's face in between your thighs, try lying on your side to have oral sex, instead. Turn onto either side and bring your thighs in toward your chest—keeping your feet stretched out a bit in front of you. This provides your spouse access to your vulva and anus—giving them two regions to explore—while keeping you more comfortable.

Tips

1. GO FOR BASIC WITH A LIE-DOWN POSITION
While he's positioned on his back, approach his manhood with your mouth by:

Going for his penis from the side, so that your body is virtually perpendicular to his

Kneel, kneel in front of him, or lie on your belly between his spread legs
Lie on your stomach or kneel alongside his body, practically in a 69 position, but with your body beside his rather than on top,

with your chest resting on his lower abdomen

2. GIVE HIM CONTROL WITH AN OPEN MOUTH AT THE BEDSIDE
Lay on your back on the bed with your head at the extreme edge of the mattress, while he stands and controls the movements.

This position may be obtained with the provider either face-up or face-down, both of which have their benefits.

3. GRAB A CHAIR FOR DOUBLE THE ORAL POSITION FUN
A chair is a creative oral sex accessory when it comes to fulfilling him.

Either have him take a seat while you kneel on the floor in front of him (grab a cushion for your knees to feel cozier) or you have a seat while he puts himself in front of your face.

Oral Sex Techniques To WOW Your Male Partner

Men's genitals are more complex than they got credit for, even though his parts are nowhere near as difficult to stimulate as a female's.
Pleasing a guy with the best oral sex techniques is all about learning what regions need the most attention.

Check out these oral sex suggestions for him.

How to pleasure a man with oral sex.

1.Do Some Teasing With Your Tongue First
If he's not quite entirely aroused or even if you just want to get things off to a slow

start, start by teasing him with the tip of your wet tongue.

Glide and flick your tongue along the length of his shaft, around his frenulum, or even his scrotum.
Slowly trace your fully opened tongue up to his head and then circle it with your tongue.
Slow and steady teasing develops anticipation for what's to come, which may be immensely exhilarating for him.
2. Keep Your Hands Involved
Sexual demonstration with a banana
Utilizing your hands and fingers to touch, fondle, and squeeze while using your mouth is ever-important when it comes to oral sex for males.

3. Give His Testicles And Scrotum Some Attention
Testicle and scrotum play are vital elements of oral sex for guys, although it's typical to neglect this fact.

Even while the scrotum and testicles are not loaded with as many nerve endings as his penis, playing with them may promote blood circulation to his genitals and aid with ejaculate output.

Not to mention, he's going to appreciate it as you build up his enjoyment.

The BIGGEST Rules of Scrotum and Testicle Play

Be gentle, whether fondling, squeezing, or sucking. Tread softly so you don't bring him unwanted harm.
Do what he loves. Some males appreciate this activity during oral sex more than others. If you're uncertain, ask him first.
Take off cumbersome jewelry, be cautious with fingernails, and monitor your teeth,

since they might cut or harm this sensitive skin and tissue.

If you're new to orally pleasuring his testicles, perform some mild tongue flicking and lapping, and maybe some ever-soft kissing and sucking.

4. Increase Pace And Intensity As He Gets Closer To Climax

When you sense that he is coming near to climax, if you want him to reach that point, gradually ramp up intensity and tempo with whatever it is you're doing that's providing him pleasure.

For example, if you're sucking and stroking, do it with a little more pressure and a little quicker. But develop him up gently.

A key here is to retain your beat.

Don't modify your action too abruptly unless you're attempting to guide him away from orgasming right then (e.g. moving from sucking and stroking to flicking your tongue down his shaft) (e.g. switching from sucking and stroking to flicking your tongue along his shaft).

5. Talk To Him
Seductive lady eager for oral sex
Ask what guys desire with oral sex, and you'll receive several replies.

But there's one thing that you can very much bet on: he's going to like your vocal contribution.

Whether you're asking him what he enjoys or telling him what you're doing while you're doing it and how much you're enjoying yourself, he's going to be happy with your compliments.

And of course, talking nasty during any form of sexual activity doesn't hurt, either.

Plus, chatting during oral sex and foreplay helps you become acquainted with what he appreciates the most.

Takeaways

Oral sex may be like the opening act that sets the scene for the full sexual performance. It also doesn't even have to be a preparation for intercourse - it's a lot of joy to give and receive for both persons involved. Remember:

Communicate. Ask questions. Verbalize.
Check your inhibitions at the entrance
Because oral sex is up-close and intimate.
Keep your hands engaged.
All oral sex recipients might have distinct preferences.
Start gradually to generate anticipation.
Familiarize yourself with your partner's physique.

Have fun!
While it seems like it would be simple to do things wrong, oral sex is not rocket science.

With a little coaching, open conversation with your partner, and maybe even a little trial and error, oral sex transforms everything... for the better!

Chapter 4:

Oral sex myth

Oral sex might appear puzzling if you think about it when you're not fired on. You're meant to place your mouth where? And you would like someone's face in your most intimate region why? But at the moment, when you're with someone you're like, oral sex might feel like a more clever innovation than the lighting. The only difficult aspect is when you're having sex with a man and some blow job misconceptions stand in the way of both of you enjoying the deed as much as possible. Here, are 13 blow job misconceptions you should quit believing, immediately.

1. Myth: You should swallow even if you're not a fan.

Unlike green smoothies, semen is not some nutrient-rich elixir. When you treat someone to a mouth-induced orgasm, they don't get to criticize what you do after the event. Spit, swallow, get out of the way so it doesn't go in your hair, whatever. As long as you're not like, "Ew, this is terrible, you're a beast," there shouldn't be any complaints.

2. Myth: All men are obsessed with blowies, so if a dude doesn't want one, he hates you.
There are so many reasons a guy may not be up for a blow job. Just as some women adore getting oral sex and others like alternative sorts of clitoral amusement, he can be into a different style of foreplay. Or he may be sparing you from confronting his sweaty post-workout package. Or maybe he wants to chat about his emotions instead of having sex. Point is, it doesn't inherently imply he doesn't like you or thinks your blow jobs are horrible.

3. Myth: Deep-throating is the key to an excellent BJ.
If you can deep throat without trouble, go for it. It's a wonderful ability that you sadly can't include on your résumé, so utilize it when you can. But you may also provide a superb blow job without the head of a penis aggravating your gag reflex.

4. Myth: There's only one blow job position.
There's a whole broad universe of oral sex positions out there beyond you kneeling in front of him. You may try 69, laying next to him, your head dangling over the bed, lying down while he kneels on top of you, and so much more.

5. Myth: A blow job isn't "real sex."
For some women, being face-to-face with a penis is more personal than having PIV intercourse. And even if you're not one of them, you can still catch sexually transmitted illnesses by giving a blow job since you're sharing body fluids (and you

can also get STIs like herpes and HPV via skin-to-skin contact) (and you can also get STIs like herpes and HPV from skin-to-skin contact).

6. Myth: It's normal for guys to push your head down.
Great if it turns you on. But if it makes you feel awkward, ask him to stop. Blow jobs should be nice for both persons, not just the one getting them.

7. Myth: If your teeth touch his penis, it'll fall off.
The world won't end when you encounter a little teeth-penis touch. As long as you're not scraping them up and down his shaft throughout, it's probably not a problem. Depending on the man, he could even appreciate it! But ask before doing it purposefully.

8. Myth: You always have to execute a blow job to completion.

You could. Or you could swap off, so he goes down on you for a little, then you continue giving him a blow job after. Or you might stop before he comes and continue sex till he orgasms. Or you might break up intercourse with several sessions of oral sex. The final aim doesn't necessarily have to be the climax.

9. Myth: Your mouth can always supply enough spit to make the deed delightful.
Cottonmouth occurs. Luckily, flavored lube exists! Just be sure to choose a sort that's compatible with condoms if they're a part of your sex routine, and also ensure that it's safe for intercourse if you intend on doing that after.

10. Myth: If your BJ abilities are up to standard, it should be over in a few minutes.
So many things may impact how much time it takes a guy to orgasm: when he most recently came, what he's thinking about, if

he's holding back because he wants it to continue longer...

11. Myth: You need blow-job wizardry for uncircumcised penises.
An uncircumcised penis is still encased in its foreskin, which covers the head. A circumcised penis no longer has a foreskin, therefore the head is visible. That's the only difference—they're still penises, and males still appreciate it when you touch them.

Yes, the two forms frequently demand different sorts of stimulation, as uncircumcised penises sometimes have more sensitive heads and there's more skin to play with. But if you're accustomed to one type of penis and meet another, don't panic. Just ask the man what he loves! You hold his penis in your hands. He probably won't mind if you ask just how he'd want you to handle it.

12. Myth: If you give your mouth a rest, you have to start from the beginning.

If he's right on the edge of orgasm and you call a time-out, sure, you'll probably have to put in some more effort to bring him back to the point of no return. But if you feel like your jaw's seizing up, give it a break. You may use your hands to keep the nice emotions continuing.

13. Myth: You have to enjoy giving blow jobs to be attractive.

You know that whole concept of how nothing's sexier than a lady who loves giving blow jobs so much, she can nearly climax from them? False. Enthusiasm is always beautiful, but you don't have to worship at the blow job shrine to be attractive yourself.

Chapter 5:

Safe oral sex

Oral sex and STIs
Oral sex is when someone stimulates the genitals of another person with their mouth. It is crucial to perform safe oral sex to avoid contracting a sexually transmitted infection (STI) (STI).

If you suffer mouth sores after delivering oral sex, it is crucial to seek medical help.

Oral intercourse is one of the most prevalent ways that sexually transmitted diseases (STIs) are passed on. STIs that may be caught during oral sex are:

chlamydia\sgonorrhoea
herpes\sgenital warts
hepatitis (A, B, and C) (A, B, and C)
HIV\ssyphilis

If you feel that you may have a sexually transmitted infection (STI), it is crucial to consult your doctor, local family planning clinic, or sexual health clinic, as soon as possible.

Preventing STIs
You may avoid contracting STIs during oral sex by making sure that your partner wears a condom or a dental dam.

A dental dam, which is a thin piece of latex, may also be worn during oral intercourse to prevent the transmission of infection. It may be put over the genitals or anus (back passage) before giving oral sex. It forms a barrier that stops body fluids from being exchanged between persons and minimizes your chance of having a sexually transmitted illness.

If you offer oral sex, be sure you don't have sores, wounds, gum disease, ulcers, cuts, herpes, or infections in your mouth. It's crucial to make sure your tongue and gums are in excellent shape before you offer oral sex.

Another approach to lowering the risk of an STI is by avoiding allowing your spouse to ejaculate (come) into your mouth.

Looking after your mouth
Here are some tips on how to care for your mouth:

You should strive to restrict the number of sugary meals and beverages that you consume. Have them as an occasional treat.
Make sure you brush your teeth twice a day using fluoride toothpaste to decrease the build-up of germs in your mouth. Gently brush your gums and tongue as well.
If you wear dentures, ensure sure they are cleaned correctly and that the skin beneath the dentures is likewise clean. Rinse your mouth out after every meal.

Smoking might also increase oral infections. If you smoke, attempt to cut down or stop smoking.

It's crucial to see your dentist at least once a year. Consider getting your teeth cleaned sometimes by a hygienist.

Avoid oral intercourse if you have sores or ulcers in your mouth or around your lips.

If you are in pain, obtain guidance on drugs you can take.

www.ingramcontent.com/pod-product-compliance
Lightning Source LLC
Chambersburg PA
CBHW061258140726
47998CB00006B/2258